GREAT WAYS
TO SABOTAGE
A GOOD CONVERSATION

PAUL W. SCHENK, PSY.D.

STANDARD PRESS

© 2002

Great Ways to Sabotage a Good Conversation / Paul Schenk

ISBN 0-9720178-0-1

I. Title.

Printed in the United States of America

First Edition

1 2 3 4 5 6 7 8 9 10

Book design by Sherie Watkins Design, Inc., 1449 Cornell Rd., Atlanta, GA 30306

ARLENE S. PIPKIN
1942 - 2002

I dedicate this book to my sister, Arlene, who continued to be a wonderful role model to so many throughout her life. Even as she shared one final dance with metastatic breast cancer, she celebrated life, savoring even the opportunities embedded in times of crisis, radiating grace and joy to all who had the good fortune to meet her.

April 8, 2002
Paul W. Schenk, Psy.D.

ACKNOWLEDGMENTS:

A number of people have contributed in varied ways to the development and realization of this book. In this small way, I wish to convey my grateful appreciation to my wife, Cheryl, and our two sons, Michael and Matt, both for their support and their willingness to forgive the many hours that my writing took away from family time; to my colleague, Bill Doverspike, Ph.D., for both his editing expertise and his many words of encouragement; to Angela Ebron, my editor at Family Circle, for her gentle, constructive mentoring; to Joe Sinclair and Jeff Lewis at New Learning, for helping provide an ongoing incentive to continue expanding the ideas presented here; to Walker Pipkin, Ph.D., my brother-in-law, for his timely affirmations; to Sherie Watkins for her gifted way of weaving playfulness into the layout; and to my clients for entrusting me with so many personal stories over the years.

TABLE OF CONTENTS

INTRODUCTION

When I began working as a psychologist nearly 25 years ago, I never thought I'd spend much time focusing on language. Sure, I knew I'd be listening to people talk about the problems they were having. But I tend to think visually – I get mental "pictures" of what people are saying. So it came as a real surprise when I found myself consistently hearing clients use the same dozen or two words to describe problems in their lives and in their relationships. More importantly, I noticed that those words were actually language traps, creating the problems they were describing. When people quit using these language traps, many of the problems disappeared or became much more manageable.

©Baby Blues Partnership

This book provides a guide for improving your relationships and how you feel about yourself. How? By showing you how to make a few small changes in the ways you think and talk. But if it's that easy, it can't make that much of a difference, right? The catch is that it's not that easy to make these "simple" language changes. Habits are hard to change, including those that involve how you use words to communicate.

At first, most people don't even recognize how much their day-to-day speech is peppered with language traps. I'll show you ways to have some fun training your ears to notice them. But I'll warn you, you may hate me for it at first. Once you begin to notice these words, you're likely to feel bombarded by them as you hear how often they are used and you realize how effectively the speaker is unwittingly sabotaging a good conversation. One client put it roughly this way:

"When you first started talking about this language stuff I thought you were just being incredibly nitpicky. Then I decided to check it out for myself. For years I've had one girl friend that I'm really comfortable talking with in a way that I'm not with my other friends. As I listened carefully to how each of my friends talks, I realized she's the only one who doesn't use those words you've been talking about! That's when I had to admit maybe you were on to something."

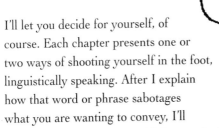

I'll let you decide for yourself, of course. Each chapter presents one or two ways of shooting yourself in the foot, linguistically speaking. After I explain how that word or phrase sabotages what you are wanting to convey, I'll give you simple ways to avoid that particular language trap. Sometimes it just takes substituting another word; sometimes it's a matter of rearranging a few words.

For the most part, it is not important to read the chapters in sequence. Choose one that catches your interest and read it. Then spend a few days listening for those words in everyday conversations. Play with the suggestions I offer for eliminating this language trap and decide for yourself what difference they make. When you're ready, select another chapter and repeat the process. Go slowly. Be gentle and patient with yourself. Avoid the common mistake of new exercise enthusiasts who completely abandon a rigorous exercise schedule after a few weeks because they took on too much too quickly. Proceed in small steps. Eliminating these language traps is both easier and harder than it may seem.

I've had more than a few clients suddenly become tongue-tied and unable to complete a thought because they kept running into language traps.

There's one more reason why these language shifts can make a meaningful difference in your life. How we feel is a direct result of what we think. How we use words to think about things has tremendous impact. Advertisers know this. Press secretaries know this. Real estate agents know this. There is a real estate agency in London that is very successful because it describes properties accurately. Their ads don't use phrases like, "Cozy little starter home, perfect for the fixer upper." Instead, they use language like, "Small rooms, few windows, leaky plumbing and warped floors." Prospective home buyers have come to trust that the agency will be honest with them. Each of the language traps described in this book has a subtle but powerful impact on the way you and others think about things. When you stop using words this way, you will be causing subtle but powerful shifts – positive shifts – in how you think about things. In turn, you will automatically elicit different responses from those around you. The mechanical language shifts are easy in one sense, much like using the "search and replace" feature on your word processor. What will be taking place at a deeper level is a shift in your awareness. You will find yourself confronting some core, sometimes faulty, assumptions about how relationships work – about how your own life works. Notice how well these shifts work for you. I'm confident that you'll be very pleased with the results.

Thoughts develop into words.
Words develop into deeds.
Deeds develop into habits.
Habits develop into character.
Choose your thoughts carefully.

CHAPTER 1

DON'T READ THIS CHAPTER

7:30 A.M. "Susan, don't forget to bring home your science book this afternoon. John, hurry up so you won't be late for the bus. Emily, stop running." Sound familiar? These reminders, and countless others like them, are echoed by conscientious parents in millions of homes across America every day. Every one of them comes with the good intention of helping a child avoid a problem.

So why is it that Susan is still likely to forget her science book despite the reminder?

The answer lies in the way that our brains listen to spoken language. Let me demonstrate. Imagine that I say to you, "Don't think about your left thumb." To understand what you just heard, the first thing you have to do is the one exact thing I just asked you not to do: think about your thumb! Of the millions of thoughts you could have had after my instruction, the very first one you had to have in order to understand what I said was the only thought that I didn't want you to have. Why? The brain is incapable of generating a picture of *don't*. It cannot create a picture of what it is not thinking about. It can only create images of what it is thinking about at the moment. Like those round highway warning signs with the red diagonal line through them, the word *don't* first tells the brain to create an image of the thing you are not supposed to do. Only then can it put the verbal equivalent of that red diagonal line over the idea.

| 4

But even then the picture in your head is still of the one thing you were not supposed to think about. Welcome to your first language trap. (Don't think about going back to read the introduction to the book before you continue reading this chapter.)

The real message that the brain hears from those original instructions is akin to the way children sometimes talk: Forget your science book – not. Be late for the bus – not. Run – not. Each time your child listens, the image that her brain forms is the exact opposite of what you want. Fortunately, the solution is quite simple. Instead of saying what you don't want, say what you do want: "Susan, remember to bring home your science book today. John, please get to the bus stop on time. Emily, please walk."

Words like *don't* and *stop* do have their usefulness. They are very helpful in identifying for your child the exact behavior which you want her to change or avoid. For example, "Don't touch the stove. It's hot." However, teaching safety and good social skills involves communicating alternatives as well. For example, no one would argue with the importance of teaching a young child, "Don't run into the street. You might get hit by a car." However, it is equally important to teach children how to deal safely with traffic. To do this, a parent can follow the earlier caution with, "Please hold my hand while we look both ways so we can cross the street safely." After focusing on what not to do, the parent tells the child what she wants him to do.

In my clinical work, I find that when parents begin to practice this simple language change, they often get tongue-tied for awhile. I suspect this is because with our busy lifestyles, much of the parenting that we do feels like putting out brush fires.

"Tim, please stop bothering your sister." "Janie, stop whining."
Unfortunately, these interventions often only add fuel to the fires.
Tim's brain just heard his mother say, "Please bother your sister –
not." Janie's brain heard her father say, "Whine – not." For many
parents, the ease of figuring out an alternative behavior that they
can live with seems inversely proportional to how tired they are.

It is easy to identify annoying behavior. But
sometimes I find that parents get momentarily
tongue-tied searching for what to say next.
Some behaviors have opposites which are
easy to articulate, for example, "Don't run.
Please walk." But what is the verbal opposite
of whining? Sometimes I have to settle for an
approximation such as, "Janie, please talk to
me in a nicer tone of voice."

> **A "don't" experiment
> to do with a friend or
> colleague:**
> While facing each
> other in a public place
> like a restaurant,
> gesture with a glance
> over the person's
> shoulder and say,
> "Don't look now,
> but..." Notice what
> the other person
> does next.

It is one thing to agree that this simple change
makes sense. However, it is quite another thing to
actually implement it. This is because people stop noticing behaviors
which have become habits. It is difficult to change what you say if you
don't even notice that you are saying it. The first step is to train your
ear to notice words like *don't* and *not*. This is easier to do with someone
else's language than your own. I find that a fun and easy way to do
this is to sit with your child or teenager while he watches a program
like Rug Rats or Malcolm in the Middle. Listen to how the adults talk
to the children (or even other adults.) Notice how many times you
can catch words like *don't*.

Then, just for fun, notice the outcome of each of those *don'ts*.
When you begin to catch your own use of *don't*, be gentle with
yourself. After all, you probably had years of role modeling from
your own parents, plus your own years of practice. When you catch
a *don't*, just follow it with what you do want your child to do. For
example, "Jason, don't forget your lunch money. Please be sure it's
in your lunch bag." Remember, the goal is not (did I say *not?*)
to eliminate the use of such words, only to be sure that you also
clearly convey what you do want your child to do.

©Baby Blues Partnership

To Should
or Not to Should
is the Wrong Question

Ah, those well intentioned tidbits of self-directed advice: "I should get more exercise." "I shouldn't have any dessert tonight." "I should call my mother." Whether the verb is *should* or one of the others in the box below, I find the effect is routinely counter-productive. *Shoulds* rarely produce the intended result. Worse than that, the emotional past tense of *should* is either guilt or resentment. If I don't do what I should do, I'll feel guilty; but if I do what I should do, I'll feel resentful. To understand how this works, let's take a closer look at why I ask my clients to carefully avoid *shoulding* on themselves.

**Verbs with similar effects
to *should*:**

**supposed to
ought to
have to
got to
need to***

*often functions like *should*,
though not always

It has been my experience that most parents often convey personal and societal expectations about behavior using *should* language. "You should have been in bed an hour ago." "You shouldn't hit your brother." "You should have told me last night you needed that blouse for school today." The intent is at least benign if not purely positive: to teach children values, good relationship skills, effective living skills, and so forth. So what happens to make this simple idea backfire?

©Baby Blues Partnership

Implied in the grammatical structure of a parental *should* is an ambiguity about whether these are your personal values or some universal standard.

For example, "One should chew with his mouth closed." Children are expected to comply because of the hierarchical authority in the parent-child relationship, whether or not they agree with the *should*. While your children may try to argue the point with you, with whom do adults argue when they *should* on themselves? When a parent and child debate the question, it is a debate between two people. When adults use an internalized *should* on themselves, they create an internal power struggle that takes on the following basic form: "Am I going to do what someone else thinks I *should* do or am I going to do what I want to do?" The power struggle hinges on a subtle question about who gets to cast the tie-breaking vote, which gets interesting when the power struggle is an internal one!

But there's another factor that gives a *should* its additional clout. I only *should* on myself if I agree in part, but not completely, with the *should*. For example, "I *should* go to bed but I want to stay up and watch the rest of this movie." I agree with the *should*, in part, because it makes sense for me to get a good night's sleep, but I also want to watch the movie. Because I partially accept the principle embedded in the *should*, I will feel guilty if I don't honor it. Note that if I completely accepted the principle, I wouldn't use *should* as the verb. I would simply go to bed. Since I like to see myself as a man with good principles, guilt is the price I pay for clinging to an image of myself when I'm not living up to it. Guilt is an ineffective tool for image management that fools neither me nor those around me. Notice that guilt comes in various sizes: a small *should* produces a small guilt; a big *should* produces big guilt.

Guilt is the price you pay for clinging to an IMAGE of yourself when you're not living up to it.

Why not just comply with the *should?* Compliance with a *should* produces resentment. Resentment can be thought of as anger directed at someone else for a decision I'm not owning as my own. If I *should* stay late at work because the boss wants me to finish a project, I will resent the boss for "making me" stay late when the actual choice to do so was my own.

(*Make me's* are the topic of Chapter 6. For now, consider that the use of *make me* masks the awareness of other options, such as my assumption that the boss would get very angry with me if I don't stay late.) In the same way, *shoulds* directed at others can be thought of as premeditated resentment. If the other person does not do what you think they *should* do, you are likely to feel resentful in proportion to the impor- tance you attach to the *should*. For example, "My son should remember to do his chores without my reminding him" will lead to my feeling resentful towards him when he doesn't comply.

©Zits Partnership

Expectations are premeditiated resentment.

Fortunately, there is a simple linguistic solution to the trap inherent in *shoulds*. Begin by defining both what the *should* is and what it is that you *want* to do. Then substitute the word *want* for the word *should*. The resulting template looks like this:

I should do X, but I want to do Y.
I want to do X, and I also want to do Y.

The first sentence pits your self-image against an unknown, external adversary, that is, whose *should* is it? The second sentence involves an internal choice between two competing personal wants. Now image management is no longer the issue. You're left with the simple reality that you want to do two things that are mutually incompatible. Either way, you're going to have to live with a trade-off, and either way you will automatically own responsibility for the choice. There can be no guilt or resentment as an after-effect. If you choose, you can still be annoyed that your two wants are incompatible, but you will be able to feel good about whichever one you finally choose to enact. Some nights I watch the rest of the movie; some nights I go to bed – guilt free in either case.

©Zits Partnership

When I introduce my clients to the idea of guilt as a consequence of *should*, many of them raise a valid question about the function of guilt in society. Shame and feeling ashamed are long-standing tools in society's efforts to get its members to comply with culturally based values. But whereas shame, regret, and remorse seem to function as effective motivators for behavioral change, I find that guilt seldom does. Let's look at how guilt serves as an image management tool. Let's assume you want to be a member of the Good Parents Club. Like many clubs, this one has two levels of membership. To be a Class A member, you must follow every rule of the club all of the time. For example, one rule of the Good Parents Club is, "Never yell at your children." Since Class A membership has some rather tough standards, Class B membership is also an option. You can remain a member of the Good Parents Club as long as you feel guilty whenever you do yell at your children. Class B members can be recognized by such comments as, "I'm not really the kind of parent who yells at my child, but . . . (fill in an excuse with a tone of implied guilt.)" It's much easier to be a Class A member of the Good Enough Parents Club. This club has rules like, "Seldom yell at your children."

Where guilt is the past tense of *should*, I would suggest that shame, regret, and remorse are the past tense of shall. Guilt seldom works to change behavior in a constructive way. By contrast, I find that shame, regret, and remorse are effective at changing future behavior. Notice that when God gave the 10 commandments to Moses, the verb used was *shall*, not *should*. Moses understood these were moral imperatives, not optional guidelines. I find there is no image management associated with feeling ashamed or remorseful the way there is with guilt.

This distinction between the two verbs has carried over into America's legal code where laws are typically written using the verb *shall,* which means compliance is imperative, or *may,* which permits but does not require compliance. Legislators don't use *should* when they draft laws. Perhaps they recognize that to do so would be to ask the courts to merely impose a sentence of feeling guilty for those who violate a *should* law.

©Baby Blues Partnership

When you *should* on yourself or another person, think of it as committing premeditated guilt or resentment. The next time you start to ask yourself, "What should I do?" picture a chorus of my clients grinning as they playfully admonish, "You shouldn't *should* on yourself!" Keeping a sense of humor will be very helpful as you begin to notice how frequently people advise themselves (and others) with the *should* family of verbs. Linguistic awareness is not always music to the ears. However, I will predict that exchanging your *shoulds* for a healthier awareness of your own competing wants will be well worth the effort.

**Replace
"I *should*" with**

I want to_____
I choose to_____

12

©Zits Partnership

TIME FOR BED NOW, OKAY?

Children seem to learn our bad linguistic habits faster than the multiplication tables. The problem is primarily a developmental one at first. From about ages 4 through 11, children go through an extended stage of "concrete thinking" which is characterized by understanding the world around them in rather black-and-white terms. They listen and think quite literally about things, and have much less ability to deal with subtleties or abstract concepts. For example, there is a story of a child who became hysterical when his parents explained how the surgeon would "put him to sleep" to remove his tonsils. He begged them not to let the doctor kill him like the veterinarian had done to their aging family pet the year before.

©Baby Blues Partnership

Unfortunately, by the time children have moved into the stage of abstract thinking as teenagers, most have developed a number of bad linguistic habits which are quite capable of surviving well into parenthood. Like the other language traps discussed in this book, the one in this chapter routinely triggers argumentative or oppositional behaviors in children. The solution to the trap utilizes your children's natural style of thinking to help them understand what you really want. Modeling good linguistic habits will elicit better cooperation in the same way that "please" and "thank you" do.

Most language traps seem evenly distributed between mothers and fathers with the exception of this one: "Okay" is the most common word that I find mothers use with children to conclude a request. For example, "It's time for bed now, okay?" In their efforts to be democratic, mothers routinely turn such a request from a statement into a question with the addition of the final word. The question actually asks the child to think about whether she wants to stop playing and go to bed. Her brain hears the question as, "Do you want to go to bed now?" It is the rare child who will answer "yes" to such a question. Most children answer in a way that conveys, "Of course not!" A common variation on this theme is the "Would you like to. . ." request. For the concrete thinking child the question, "Would you like to help me set the table?" literally asks him to think about whether he would like to do that. Care to predict the answer most children will give?

The use of *okay* and *would you* language tells your child she has a choice, which is not what you intended. Children get angry at what I call "pseudo-democracy" situations like this. A few are brave enough to say what they're thinking: "Why did you ask me for my opinion

> **Avoid using "…, okay?" and "would you…?" unless it's really okay for your child to answer "no."**

if you've already made up your mind?" When the behavior requested of the child is mandatory and not optional, the solution is to avoid turning such statements into questions. Simply leave off the word *okay*. For example, "It's time for bed." "Please come help set the table." In practice I find it is often easier to substitute a different word for *okay* so that the sentence remains a question. For example, "It's time for bed now, understand?" It is much easier for a child to answer "yes" to this question as it only asks if he understands what was just said. It no longer asks for his consent. But the question also invites the child's cooperation.

Making the changes I've suggested is easier to do once you train your ears to listen for the language traps. This can be a family project that most children enjoy because I find they love catching their parents using these traps.

One way to help everyone learn to listen for these words – and to notice the unintended consequences – is to have the family watch an evening sitcom together. If you videotape it first, you can rewind the tape to help everyone notice the trigger words and the results. Take turns using the solutions I've proposed here to let everyone get some practice. As you learn to convey more clearly what you really want, you'll avoid traps like these which cause friction between you and your children. Because young children listen carefully but literally at this age, it is critical that we listen to our own language as well as our children do.

CHAPTER 4

ABSOLUTELY EFFECTIVE WAYS TO SABOTAGE A GOOD CONVERSATION

hen one of my sons was five years old, he went through a phase of frequently complaining with a classic double absolute, "You *never* let me have *any* fun!" As a father who is also a clinical psychologist, I initially experimented with a few time honored parental responses to be sure they wouldn't work. First the sarcastic response: "Yea, right, I never take you anywhere." Then, I tried the "How could you say that?" wounded parent response: "What?! I'm always taking you here for ice cream, there for something to eat, or to the mall to look around." Finally the "I'll show you" response: "Fine, then don't plan on asking me to take you to Subway for dinner this Tuesday like we always do." I was right: they didn't work. Here's why.

The problem with absolutes

Absolute words literally mean that there's not even a single exception. (See the first column in the table on the next page.) Once again, the first problem with such words stems from how the brain listens. Put simply, your brain tends to listen literally. This is particularly true in children from ages four to 11 who are in the stage of concrete thinking, but I find it is usually just as true in adults. Consider the following example: "Sarah, you never hang up your coat." If Sarah has hung up her coat even once, then her parent's accusation is false.

16

Having learned that it is important to tell the truth, Sarah will promptly seek to correct her parent by pointing out at least one exception. From here the conversation usually deteriorates into an argument about percentages. Lost is her parent's original intent to have Sarah hang up her coat more often.

Absolute	Relative
Never, ever	seldom, rarely, infrequently
always	often, usually
everybody	most, a lot
nobody	few, some, a couple of
any	some, a little

There are additional problems with absolute language. They are usually used as criticism without offering a specific solution for the problem. As such, the focus is on the negative. Further, the emotional tone which accompanies their use is often experienced as an attack on the whole person, not just the specific behavior. What kind of parents want to be told that they never let their children have any fun? There is an implied character attack in accusations of the absolute type. If you are the target of this kind of attack, then you have a dual task. Not only do you have to point out exceptions that prove the accusation is false, but you also have to defend your character by proving that the implied accusation is also false. I suspect the resulting escalation in the intensity of the conversation has more to do with this implicit attack on character than with the specific behavior in question. To make matters even worse, parents often sense their child is attempting manipulation by guilt. For example, if Susie complains, "You let Janie get away with everything," her mother may hear this as, "You shouldn't let Janie get away with everything." (Now that you've read Chapter 2, though, you can avoid the *should* trap.)

The solution

Fortunately, the solution to the language trap of
absolutes is quite simple. To avoid an argument
over the exceptions, replace the absolute word with
a relative word. (See the second column in the table at
left.) Such words allow for a gray area. The brain has a
much easier time with words like *often* than it does with
always. A relative word like *often* allows the speaker and
listener to have different personal definitions. Just how frequently
does something have to occur to be called *often?* More importantly,
you can focus on the solution rather than the problem. For example,
instead of saying, "You seldom pick up your dirty clothes," you
can say, "I would like you to put your dirty clothes in the hamper
more often."

Reducing how often you speak in absolutes is much easier to do
once you train your ears to listen for their varied forms. As with the
other language traps, have fun involving your kids. Invite them to
catch you using absolutes. Post a list of absolute words for a week or
two to help remind them what words to listen for. In my office, I playfully award bonus points to clients who catch other family members
using multiple absolutes in a single sentence. Another way to help
everyone learn to listen for these words – and to notice the unintended
consequences – is to use the suggestion I gave at the end of Chapter 3.
Videotape an evening sitcom. Let the family listen for absolute
language traps. Notice what happens in the sitcom right after each
trap occurs. Take turns substituting relative words for the absolutes
to let everyone get some practice. As one way to get the whole family
involved, let everyone read the sample sentences in the box on the
following page. Then go in a circle and let each person add his or
her own example.

Cracking The Code

When you say:	What the child really hears/thinks:	Instead say:
You're always watching TV.	Do I ever do anything else? Duh, of course! There you go exaggerating again.	I would like you to spend more time (reading, playing, etc.)
Don't you ever listen to what I'm telling you?	You mean like when you're whining at me like this?	Please listen carefully to what I'm about to say.
I've never seen messier homework.	You should see the stuff I threw away last week.	I want you to write more neatly.
You never turn off the lights.	That's not true. I turned out the bathroom light last night.	Please remember to turn off the lights more often.
Don't you have anything better to do?	This seems to be annoying you just fine.	I would like you to stop playing video games now and go play outside for awhile.

You *never* let me have any fun.

How did I finally deal with my five year old's double absolutes? I used my knowledge of how absolutes work to our mutual advantage:

 Matt: You never let me have any fun.

Dad: (Said calmly with a tone of slight resignation as if he'd just caught me being a bad parent.) You're right Matt. I never take you to Subway. I never take you to the mall. I never play catch with you.

 Matt: Yes you do! (Said with an incredulous tone implying, "What are you saying? Of course you do those things with me!" thus proving my absolutes and his to be false.)

Dad: What would you like to do together right now that will be fun?

 Matt: How about if we go shoot some baskets?

If Matt had been much older, I probably would have had to use a different strategy. As it was, by carefully avoiding any hint of sarcasm in my voice, this worked fine. For older children and adults, here's a generic solution you can use when someone directs an absolute at you. I want to warn you, though. This one takes a lot more practice because you are intercepting your own reaction to a language trap which has already occurred, rather than avoiding the language trap in the first place. When you hear the absolute, make a mental substitution of a relative term. For example, suppose your teenager gripes that you are always complaining to him about something. Mentally translate this to, "You often complain to me about something." It helps if you can agree that the particular relative term you substituted is reasonably accurate. At this point you can respond, "You're right, I often complain to you." Most people, even teenagers, won't quibble about your substituting often for always. This leaves the door open for you and your teenager to begin to negotiate a specific change on the issue that triggered the gripe.

With family members, you can also agree to work together to use fewer absolutes. With colleagues at work, you may decide it is safer to resist the temptation to point out their use of language traps. You can sidestep the unintended sabotage and still keep the conversation going if you silently make the mental substitution and focus on what the speaker would like you to do more, or less, often. For example, suppose a colleague tells you, "I can never find you when I need to ask you a question." You might respond, "I am often hard to reach, aren't I? Apparently that's more of a problem for you than I realized. Let's consider some alternatives that might work better for both of us."

Of all the language traps that I hear family members use on each other in my office, the absolutes are among the best at derailing an otherwise good conversation. By triggering an immediate objection from the listener, the speaker's original intent is quickly lost in the defensive tone of the conversation that follows. Now you have another subtle, yet powerful, strategy for keeping your conversations on track. Whether you are the speaker or the listener, you can avoid or sidestep absolute language traps at home if you'll remember to do what one client wisely punned, "Use relatives with relatives."

Use "relatives" with relatives.

CHAPTER 5

WHY *WHY* DOESN'T WORK

Why is the sky blue, Daddy?" "Why aren't you in bed, son?" "Why don't you try it this way?" Each of these questions offers a different use of why. The first, though often part of a litany of *why* questions, begins with an innocent curiosity from a child eager to learn about the world. The other two uses are effective ways to sabotage a good conversation. Let's take a look at why conversations might be a lot better off if children were the only people allowed to use the word *why*.

The curious *why*

The young child's use of *why* usually reflects curiosity about the world. As the opening word to a question, *why* indicates a desire to learn, to better understand how things work. Even when the question may prove socially awkward, such as "Why does that man have no hair?" the child's motivation is simply one of seeking to learn. I find that what makes these questions difficult for many parents is that they discover they often do not know the answer. Rather than deal with that fact directly, many parents request that the

©Baby Blues Partnership

child stop asking why. The unfortunate effect is to stifle curiosity. Far more helpful would be a response which acknowledges, "I don't know why the sky is blue. Let's see how we might find out the answer to the question."

The angry *why*

When adults get hold of the word *why*, they seem to have the ability to strip it of its innocence. When adults ask a question which begins with *why*, the tone is often one of irritation or annoyance. For example, "Why isn't your homework done?" On paper these words seem innocent enough. The punctuation mark at the end of the question does little to convey the larger meaning. To convey the critical emotional tone in which most adults ask the question *why*, what would be needed is both a "?" and a "!" at the end of the sentence: "Why isn't your homework done?!" Literally, of course, the sentence is a question. The child knows this and also knows that when a parent asks a question, the child is expected to answer it. However, the tone of the question lets the child know that the true message the parent wants to convey is, "I don't really care why your homework isn't done. I just want you to know that I'm mad that it isn't done." Thus the child has a real dilemma. He must answer a question when Mom has already implied she doesn't care about the answer. Further, if he answers the question truthfully, he knows he will be in even more trouble. What child will openly admit to a parent, "I didn't do my homework because I was having more fun playing"?

©Zits Partner

The child's solution to this dilemma is often to experiment with giving plausible excuses. The child knows he is lying in offering such excuses, but hopes that the parent will not realize this is the case. Little does the parent realize that he is undermining his relationship with his child by creating such a scenario in which the only way the child thinks he can win is to become a convincing liar.

©Baby Blues Partnership

As with the other language traps, there is a simple way to avoid this one, too. My preferred solution is to eliminate the *why* question entirely. Instead, substitute a sentence that addresses how you're feeling about the situation, such as the homework not being done. "I'm upset that you haven't finished your homework." If you really want to hear your child's explanation, you can still ask the question. However, I recommend that you replace the word *why* with another word or phrase. For example, "What happened that your homework is not done?" "How did you decide to postpone doing your homework?" There are two reasons I prefer to do this. First, it often takes the parent a few seconds to think of a different way to ask the question. This interrupts the normal habit and gives the parent an opportunity to think about what she really wants to communicate to her child. Second, most children quickly recognize that they are in trouble when a parent begins a sentence with the word *why*. As soon as they hear the

©Baby Blues Partnership

word, they began searching for an excuse which might be effective for the current problem. Using a different word or phrase eliminates this knee-jerk response on your child's part. Moreover, if you really doesn't care why the homework isn't already done, save time and move ahead with the solution: "I'm upset that your homework isn't done yet. Please go start to work on it right now.'

Why don't you_____

The third use of the word *why* often takes the form of a three word phrase which begins a question: "Why don't you. . . ." This question is usually the second part of a brief ritual which can have any number of variations.

Here's how the sequence typically works:

What is happening:	Example
1. Mary describes a problem.	"I can't decide on a topic for this English paper I have to write."
2. Dad offers a solution.	"Why don't you write about...?"
3. Mary rejects the solution.	"I don't know anything about..." or "That's boring." or "That would take too much time."
4. Dad tries again or reacts with irritation. (Cycle back to step #2.)	"Well, then, why don't you...?"
5. Mary rejects new solution.	"I could but..." (Some readers will recognize this as a variation of the classic "Yes, but" way of stifling helpers.)
6. The cycle can repeat until dad leaves in frustration.	"Fine! Then you'll just have to figure out your own topic since you think none of my ideas are good enough!"

If you've read the chapters in sequence, you may already understand why this phrase often fails to produce the desired result: The human brain listens literally most of the time whether the person realizes it or not. The literal meaning of the phrase "why don't you" is "tell me all the reasons you can think of for <u>not</u> using my suggestion." In the example above, Dad offered his suggestions with the belief that they would be an effective solution to the problem. Yet by starting the sentence with a negative, he invited Mary to focus on why the advice might not work rather than focusing on why it might be the right solution. Because Dad asked for all the reasons why Mary won't use his suggestion, she responded by telling him just that! The two of them can cycle from step 4 back to step 2, or they can skip directly to the final step (6). In this final step the advice giver feels unappreciated for his efforts and the person with the problem wonders why the other person is walking away angry.

Unlike the child's use of *why* as an expression of curiosity, the context in which *why* is used here is one which stems from a different motivation. Here the speaker is motivated by wanting to be helpful. Unfortunately, *Why don't you...* elicits exactly the opposite reaction from the one which is intended. I find that a much more effective way to word the suggestion is to phrase it so that the other person thinks about how well it might work as a solution. The bulleted list below offers a few variations to get you started. Each sentence conveys an expectation of success and invites the child to mentally rehearse the proposed solution to see if he or she agrees.

- How well do you think it would work if you ...?
- What do you think would happen if you...?
- What alternatives have you already considered?
- What ideas are you still considering?
- If (insert one: time, talent, money, energy) were not an issue, what would you do?

When child-like curiosity is at the heart of your asking *why*, know that the listener is likely to respond more openly. If you have something else in mind, avoid the problems with *why* and *why don't you* by eliminating them from your speech. Play with the examples I've offered here and notice the difference.

Well, then, why don't you?

CHAPTER 6

YOU MAKE ME
SO-O-O MAD!

Sandra: "Dear, did you remember to enter that check in the checkbook?"

Jim: "No, I forgot."

Sandra: "Agghhhhh! That annoys me so-o-o much!"

Jim: "I'm s-o-r-r-r-y."

Sandra: "Right! Then how come you keep forgetting to do it?"

In this chapter, we'll take a look at a language trap that comes in several varieties, each of which can quickly derail a good conversation by unwittingly triggering a defensive response. Here are a few samples to see if you can spot the core component that defines what I call a "make me" sentence:

- "That traffic jam sure ruined my good mood this morning."
- "You hurt my feelings."
- "She makes me so mad when she assigns this much homework."
- "He ticks me off."
- "It irritates me when you do that."
- "That annoys me."

In their simplest form, *make me* sentences are amazingly efficient. They need only three words:

- a subject (e.g., you, he, she, they, that, it)
- the word "me" or "my"
- a verb that specifies what the subject does to "me."

Linguistic brevity can be a real asset, but in the case of *make me* language it is a near fool-proof recipe for sabotaging a good conversation. Whatever original intent you had will almost always take back seat to the defensive response which follows. Let's see how this happens. Then I'll offer a simple language shift that will help keep your conversations on track.

Somewhere during our early school years we learned about parts of speech such as subjects, verbs, and objects. We learned that with an active verb such as "make," the subject performs some action on the object. In this simple four word sentence, "You made me mad," the person to whom I'm speaking is 100 percent responsible for the action in the sentence. The brain interprets it just as unambiguously as it would the sentence, "You made my dinner." I am not responsible for what happened because "you" caused the action. You did it to me.

©Baby Blues Partnership

Cause and effect may be obvious where actions are concerned, but they're not always so obvious where feelings are concerned. This is because there is a critical interim step. Before you can feel you have to think. There are exceptions, of course. I'm not talking about physical feelings such as when you stub your toe. Rather, I'm talking about how you feel about people and things around you. Most events, by themselves, don't have an inherent meaning.

You decide what an event means to you. It is the meaning you attach to an event that will determine how you feel, not the event itself. Consider the following events:

- **The Dow Jones drops 200 points.**
- **Navy beats Army.**
- **The price of gasoline goes up 10%.**
- **Your teenager discovers he likes Stairway to Heaven.**
- **The forecast is for six inches of snow.**
- **You overslept this morning.**

Notice what significance or meaning you attach to each of them. Do you think your best friend, your spouse, or your teenager would attach exactly the same meaning to each event? Probably not. Feelings are spontaneous, of course. But they are spontaneous reactions to the meaning or significance you attach to an event rather than to the event itself. For example, football fans often assign a lot of meaning to a score, whereas someone who doesn't follow the game will assign little or no meaning. The same event can have very different meaning for one person than it does for someone else. In 2001, French fans were thrilled with the final score of the World Cup championship game; Italian fans left the stadium in a very different mood. They witnessed the same event and gave it a very different meaning. That's why some fans left the stadium in a very different mood. Closer to home, my son may feel relieved to finish his homework in ten minutes because it leaves him free to go play. I may feel suspicious that he finished in ten minutes because I wonder if he rushed through the assignment.

> It is the meaning you attach to an event that will determine how you feel, not the event itself.

When you use *make me* language, you skip the critical step of noticing that your feelings are the result of what you think, rather than the event itself. To the brain, *make me* language means that the event causes the feeling.

Your role in giving meaning to the event is completely missing. If the event causes the feeling, then you have no control over the situation. In other words, you have to feel that way. This implies, in turn, that the person (or thing or situation) who causes the event causes your feeling. You become helpless; the other person becomes powerful.

M*ake me* language creates not just one, but two major problems. First, you have just denied any responsibility for how you feel, having blamed someone else for making you feel that way. Yet equally problematic is the fact that you've just attacked the other person's character. Many men love Carol King's classic lyric, "You make me feel like a natural woman" because it implies the man gets all the credit. It is quite another thing to have your spouse accuse you of (intentionally) making him or her feel unimportant, hurt, or mad. Few men would like their wife to say, "You make me feel unimportant." What kind of a caring, sensitive spouse would intentionally behave that way?

©Baby Blues Partnership

It is this subtle character attack that makes what happens next very predictable. If you are the target of a make me, most of the time you will respond defensively in a way that is meant to challenge the implicit attack on your character. Whatever the original conversation was about, it will take back seat to the defense of your character or your motivations. In the opening example about the checkbook, Jim's unconvincing apology is designed to defend himself by diminishing the importance of his mistake, at the same time that his voice tone counterattacks by implying that Sandra is making far too much of the situation. Sandra's next response moves away from how she feels with an oblique attack on his motivations for forgetting. Her unspoken message is, "Apparently what is important to me doesn't matter much to you." Jim can be expected to ignore her feelings also, by continuing to defend his character and motivations in his next response. Sandra's original intent will be quickly forgotten.

The Solution

There is a simple way to avoid the *make me* language trap with its accompanying unpleasant chain reaction. A good replacement is a sentence that has three simple components: "I get _____ when you _____ because _____." Let's dissect a sample one:

I get upset when you don't enter checks in the checkbook because then I can't be sure how much money is really in the account.

The first part begins with an "I" message: "I get upset."
Here are some other examples:
- I'm mad . . .
- I felt hurt . . .
- I get annoyed . . .
- I was angry . . .

The second component describes the event which served as the catalyst: ". . .when you don't enter checks in the checkbook." The general form of this is "when you do (did)" or "when you say (said)." Here are some other examples:
- . . . when you said you couldn't make it to Janie's play at school.
- . . . when you drive so close to the car ahead.
- . . . when you wait until bed time to tell me you need something for school the next day.

The third part can take one or both of two forms. One option is to explain why it is a problem for you. For example, ". . . because then I can't be sure how much money is really in the account." The other is to offer a solution which can avoid the problem in the future. For example, "I would like to talk about some ways to avoid this problem in the future."

Here are some other examples of how it sounds when all the pieces are put together:

- I get mad when you spend so much time on the Internet because I think it means you don't want to spend time with the rest of the family.
- I become frustrated when I have to ask you to do something several times because I begin to think that what I say is unimportant to you.
- I get annoyed when you seem to rush through your home work. I would rather you take enough time to do it more carefully.
- I feel hurt when you spend so much time returning telephone calls at night. I would rather you return more of them at work the next day so that we can spend more time together.

In each of these examples, the speaker takes full responsibility for how he or she feels. In each case, "you" get a clearer picture about the meaning the other person attached to what you did. When couples practice talking this way in my office, I consistently find a marked absence of defensiveness. It is not uncommon for the other person to seem surprised upon learning how the spouse had interpreted the event. The "I" feels heard, the "you" reacts much more openly to the feedback, and together they are able to explore new alternatives for dealing with the situation.

Because feelings follow spontaneously from what you think, if you don't like how you're feeling, you can experiment with changing the meaning that you gave the event. One night a few months after our teenage son got his license, he went out to a restaurant for dinner with friends. The plan was for them to go back to the home of one of them after dinner to watch a movie. He was to call us (the worried parents of a new driver) when he arrived at the friend's house. When he had not called by 10:00 PM, my wife got mad, assuming that he had forgotten. She called him on his cell phone and learned that the group had had to wait 90 minutes to be seated for dinner and had not yet left the restaurant. With this new meaning attached to his not having called us, her anger quickly subsided.

My rule of thumb with clients is to suggest that they generate four other possible meanings of the event when they don't like how they feel. Much of the time they replace the original meaning they had given to the event with one of these new ones. This, in turn, produces a shift in feelings.

There is a poster on the wall in my office which includes the saying, "Nothing spoken when drunk that wasn't first thought out when sober." Before you can act on how you feel, your brain has to generate at least one possible response. Again, I'm not talking about "fight or flight" behavior such as what you do when you touch a hot stove. I'm talking about behavior which involves the gray matter in your brain – your thinking brain. Just as *make me* language denies our responsibility for how we feel, "the devil made me do it" language denies our responsibility for how we act. Before you can actually <u>act</u> on what you feel about what you

> **If you don't like how you're feeling, take 60 seconds to think of four different meanings you might give the event. Notice if you like one of these better than the original meaning you gave it.**

think about what happened, you have to <u>think</u> of what to do or say. In everyday life, you accomplish this thousands of times a day with lightning speed. You make dozens of minor adjustments with the steering wheel every mile to stay centered in the lane. You may quickly contemplate a variety of things you would like to say or do to the driver tailgating you. You may rehearse a number of things you'd like to tell your child when she whines, including those you swore you'd never repeat that your own mother said.

A few years ago a man came to see me for help with decision making. Before he came back for his second appointment he called me with a crisis. He was stuck in a classic "either-or" situation: He could only think of two alternative ways to handle the crisis, neither of which he liked. I asked him to take 60 seconds and think of three more possibilities. In less than a minute he rattled off three ideas.

"Do you like any of the five that you now have?" I asked him. He did, and reported it worked well when I saw him next. The same scenario happened for the next five weeks in a row. Each week for six weeks he called with a different crisis between his regular appointments. Each time he was stuck with an either-or situation. Each time I asked him to generate three more ideas. Each time he liked one of the ones he had generated. Then one week he didn't call. When he arrived for his next appointment he told me the following anecdote:

I almost called you again this week. I had another crisis. Then I thought, what is Dr. Schenk going to say? "Give me three more possibilities." So I thought of three more. What is Dr. Schenk going to say next? "Do you like one of them?" I did, so I used it. It worked, just like the others did. Then I realized I didn't call you.

With a big grin, I reached over and shook his hand. If you get stuck considering what to do next, give yourself 60 seconds to play with other possibilities. This is a place for brainstorming, for playing with fantasies, wishes and "if only's." Be sure you trust yourself to choose carefully from the ideas you generate here. You won't be held accountable for your fantasies as long as you keep them to yourself. You will be held accountable for what you actually do.

> **If you feel stuck choosing between "either-or" options, take 60 seconds to think of three additional possibilities. Often you'll find one you like better than the original ones.**

If you find that, like most people, you experience the pitfalls of *make me* language with people you care about, here is a summary of the simple steps you can take to eliminate this language trap:

1. When you hear yourself use a *make me* sentence, immediately replace the sentence with one of the "I" messages: I get _____ when you _____ because _____ and what I would prefer is . . . . It will take more than the four words of a *make me* sentence, but I promise that your original intent is much more likely to be heard.

2. If you hear yourself muttering a *make me* sentence when you
are alone, ask yourself what meaning you attached to the
event which led to this feeling. Notice that how you feel
makes sense given the meaning you gave the event. Generate
four additional meanings or interpretations of the event. If it
helps, imagine how your best friend or a close colleague might
interpret the event. Now choose from the five different
meanings. If you pick a different one, notice how your
feelings shift.

3. If you think there are no good options for what to do about
the situation, do the same thing. Generate several more
options. Allow yourself to have some fun here! Remember to
keep a tight boundary between what you think and what you
say or do. The freedom to brainstorm and fantasize wants
to be paired with sound judgment when deciding which
alternative to actually implement.

Having read this far, you may have anticipated one final point
about the *make me* language trap. Now that you know why it
triggers a defensive response, you can no longer claim involuntary
word-slaughter if you launch a counterattack to defend your
character. Now that you know how to reword a *make me* so that
the real intent comes through, you can reword any *make me* that
someone else uses on you. Now if you counterattack, you will
be guilty of choosing to commit voluntary word-slaughter.

Make me!

Finally, when you train your ear to be alert to your own use of *make me* language, you'll begin to notice how many people around you speak this way. For a time, you may find yourself reacting to each occurrence as you would to fingernails scraping on a chalkboard. Resist the strong temptation to become a self-appointed grammar teacher. Instead, use what you've learned and silently translate the other person's *make me* in your head so that it becomes an "I" message. You'll react without defensiveness and do your part to help to keep the conversation on track.

> **With practice, it will become easier to avoid committing voluntary word-slaughter.**

CHAPTER 7

DO YOU LOVE ME?

Most people appreciate the way a shift in voice tone can dramatically change the meaning of what is said. Meg Ryan demonstrates this effect in the famous pseudo-erotic restaurant scene in the movie When Harry Met Sally with the different ways she says the simple word "Yes!" Yet it also seems that most people have much less appreciation for the ways that very small shifts in the words themselves can have hidden impact in the everyday conversations couples have. Just a different pronoun or conjunction can unwittingly spark arguments and lead to hurt feelings, resentment, and anger. The same thing can happen just by turning a statement into a question. The language trap I'll discuss in this chapter has nothing to do with a couple's relationship, income or educational background. It occurs because of the hard-wired way our brains listen to what we hear. Like the traps in the previous chapters, it, too, has a simple solution.

Do you love me?

Such a simple question, short and to the point. So why is it that the common response, "Yes, of course I love you" is often wrapped in an emotional tone of puzzlement or mild annoyance that is heard as a cold contradiction of the actual words? The problem is inherent in the nature of question. Blame it, once again, on the literal way that our brains listen to questions that begin with "Do you _____." Consider the question, "Do you know the weather forecast for this weekend?" By asking you the question, I am telling you I don't already know your answer; I don't already know whether or not you know the forecast.

©Baby Blues Partnership

If I did know that your answer would be "Yes," I could skip this question and simply say, "What is the weather forecast for this weekend?" It is culturally acceptable to phrase the question the first way. Most people will understand that I have implicitly asked them to go ahead and tell me the weather forecast if they know it.

©Baby Blues Partnership

But this only works if the other person thinks it is reasonable for me not to already know the answer to the literal "Do you. . ." question. I will get in trouble if you already expect me to know your answer. If I ask my wife, "Do you love me?" I'm telling her that I'm not sure if she does. I find that when a spouse hears this question, she may quickly interpret it to mean that <u>all</u> of her prior efforts to convey her love have apparently failed miserably. Otherwise, why would he be asking? She may respond, "Yes," but her tone of voice will be anything but romantic! In turn, he comes away from the romantic opportunity with what writers Alvyn and Margaret Freed call a "cold prickly" instead of a "warm fuzzy." As they turn away from each other, she wonders what it will take to convince him of her love, and he wonders why it is so hard for her to give him a simple re-affirmation.

The solution to this language trap is easy, in part because it speaks to the *real* reason the question is usually asked in the first place. I find most spouses who pose this question know they are loved. They simply want to hear it again. Did you ever hear about the farmer's wife who laments to her husband that he never tells her that he loves her any more? He responded, "I told you the day we married." Most spouses aren't that stoic, but do tend to miss opportunities to remind their partners of their love for them.

Tell me you love me.

So instead of asking for this affirmation as a question, turn it into a statement: "Please tell me you love me." This way you convey your confidence that your spouse loves you. He or she will implicitly understand that there is no doubt about being loved; you would just like to hear it again. Maybe it would be nice if we all read minds well enough to anticipate just when our partner would like to hear those three words, "I love you," but we don't. If you want to playfully test this with your loved one, phrase it both ways a day or two apart. Notice both the words and the tone of the response you get. Also notice whether your voice tone shifts when you phrase it as a statement instead of a question. My wife did this with me when I was doing some kitchen renovations one weekend many years ago. In response to "Do you love me?" I kept working and said in a slightly irritated tone over my shoulder, "Of course I do." What followed next was classic language trap fallout. The next day she when said it the other way, "Tell me you love me," I put down my tools, wrapped my arms around her, and looked right into her eyes as I said with a mischievous grin, "Let me tell you."

Do You Want to_____

There is a variation to the "Do you_____" trap which may be surprising to some women. When a man's wife says, "Do you want to fool around tonight?" the unspoken thought many men have is, "I'm not sure. What's the right answer?" Such a man wants to be sure that the offer is being made because his wife wants to fool around, not because she thinks she <u>should</u> make the offer. (If you haven't yet read Chapter 2 which deals with *shoulds*, this reasoning may not be clear.) I have no interest in crimping the many wonderful ways that partners have of signaling each other. I only wish to reduce the occasional, unintended ambiguity in those signals for those males among us who like to get the answer right the first time.

A potentially far less risky version of this takes the form of the partner who asks, "Do you want to go out to eat tonight?" On the surface, the question only asks about your preference.

There is nothing in the wording of the question which provides a clue about whether your partner wants to go out to eat tonight. The fact that he or she may not care one way or the other does nothing to remove this uncertainty. Certainly after years of practice most of us get better at reading between the lines with our partners. But as the next section illustrates, time is not always enough. One way to avoid this ambiguity is to simply let your partner know whether you have a preference.

Do we need to talk about _____

As a psychologist, I'm not proud to admit that it took me 20 years of being married to realize that when my wife asks, "Do we need to talk about plans for the weekend?" the correct answer is "Yes." For years I had interpreted her question to mean, "Do you need to talk about plans for the weekend?" I had assumed that if she needed to talk about the plans, she would tell me so. As a result, if I didn't need to talk about the plans I would say, "No." Many wives will interpret this as a message that what they want doesn't matter. What happens next is usually not a place most husbands want to go.

> The best answer to the following type of question is usually, "yes." "Do we need to talk about...?"

There are a myriad of ways this question arises in ordinary, every-day conversation between spouses: "Do we need to talk about getting the kids to practice this week?" "Do we need to talk about the bills?" "Do we need to talk about John's progress report from school?" Almost any relationship is at risk for this language trap: spouse–spouse, parent–child, boss–employee, colleague–colleague. Again, blame this language trap on the literal way that our brains listen to language – whether or not we realize that we're doing so.

The problem here has a second component that stems from a difference in styles of decision making. Much more so than men, women use *"we"* rather than *"I"*. They phrase things in ways that are more inclusive of others. Men tend to assume other men will speak up if they have a problem with something.

On average, I find that men are more literal and less likely to read between the lines. There are two solutions to this trap. Husbands who are quick learners can avoid the problem by saying something like, "I don't need to, but would you like to talk about_____?" Alternatively, this language trap can be avoided by turning the question into a statement. Stating the simple truth about a situation seems to work much better: "Sometime this evening I would like to talk with you about our weekend plans." "Before the end of the weekend I would like us to talk with John about his progress report." Because the request is likely to be made when the other person is already involved in some other task, add a phrase that allows some flexibility while also establishing a deadline. There are numerous possibilities such as "When you're finished with the paper. . ." or "When this TV program is over. . ." or "After we put the children to bed. . ."

©Baby Blues Partnership

If you're not sure whether you're guilty of using any of these language traps at home or work, consider asking your partner or a few colleagues what they've noticed. You might give them permission to call examples to your attention when they occur so that you can train your ears to recognize the traps in real time, and then get practice changing them.

No "Ifs, Ands, or Buts"

Of all the language traps in this book, the one in this chapter is the easiest to remedy. That fact does not diminish how effectively this one word language trap can sabotage an otherwise good conversation. Perhaps its most familiar form is when it is preceded at the beginning of a sentence by the word "yes" as in "Yes, but_____." Let me use an old one-line joke to demonstrate the subtle expectations contained in the use of the word:

Well, he isn't much to look at,
but he sure has a lousy personality.

The joke works because of the word *"but"*. You expect that what follows the word will be in marked contrast to what precedes it. The second half of the sentence is a surprise because it doesn't follow this simple linguistic expectation.

The conversational damage that this word causes might be limited to the element of surprise were it not for a second implicit meaning associated with its use. It is not only that what follows in the rest of the sentence is expected to be different from what preceded it. It is that what preceded it is implicitly devalued or defined as less important than what follows. Consider this example: "John, I know we've both had a hard week and we want to take it easy this weekend, but we need to clean the house because my parents are coming." If this sentence is said to you, you're likely to think that the truth of the first half of the sentence suddenly lost most of its value as soon as you heard the word *but*.

The speaker has told you that the second half of the sentence is
more important than the first half. You may think that what you
want doesn't matter. You may feel devalued or unimportant in the
eyes of the speaker. In my work with couples I find that they often
unwittingly trigger hurt feelings with this simple word.

One of my former clients, "Jennifer", is a woman whose job at a
large HMO sometimes involved calling patients to reschedule their
appointments. As you might imagine, many of them did not take
this news particularly well. Jennifer did her best to listen politely
as patients complained about the inconvenience this was going to
cause them. "Yes, Mr. Johnson, I know this is the second time that
this has happened recently, but I need to change your appointment
time." I asked Jennifer to make one simple change in the way that
she dealt with patients in such situations. I asked her to substitute
the word *and* for the word *but.* Her first reaction was very typical
of what I see when I ask someone to do this. Her facial expression
seemed to say, "That's it? And you think that's going to make a
noticeable difference?" She humored me, though, and the next
week she had a big grin of disbelief on her face as she described
what had happened when she made the substitution.

On almost every phone call, the patient's anger seemed to dissolve when she made the switch. Here's why.

W hereas the word *but* alerts the listener to expect a change in what comes next, the word *and* builds on the linguistic notion of a "yes" set. It works like this. Start the sentence with an idea with which the listener agrees. Add a second idea with which the listener agrees, bridging the two with the word *and*. Add additional ideas if you wish, connecting each of them with the word *and*. For the listener, this develops a pattern of agreement, a "yes" set: A is true and B is true and C is true. . . . Now when you add the final phrase using *and* as the bridge word once more, you build on this "yes" set rather than negating it. Jennifer had been amazed at how easy it was. "Yes, Mr. Johnson, [echoing his complaints] I hear how frustrating this is for you and what an inconvenience it causes in your work and I wonder whether this Thursday or Friday morning at 8:30 will be better for you." In this way, Jennifer acknowledged his reality without negating it. The patients knew that they had no control over having to reschedule their appointments. In the process of rescheduling, however, they wanted to feel heard. They wanted to know that their thoughts and feelings about the situation mattered.

Let's revisit John's bad news: "John, I know we've both had a hard week and we want to take it easy this weekend and we need to clean the house because my parents are coming." John's wife no longer negates the importance of what is true for him, that he, too, has had a hard week and wants to relax this weekend. Instead, she adds two additional truths to the sentence. It is no longer an either/or situation. Substituting *and* for *but* transforms the sentence to a situation where A and B are both true. What John wants remains important.

He continues to feel valued. The shift to *and* conveys the important message that there is nothing wrong or selfish about having competing wants or wishes. He can want to relax and he can want a clean house. The fact that they may be incompatible does not make him a bad person, just a normal person with conflicting wants!

Yes, but…!

Using *and* to create an expectation of agreement in this way can be helpful in a variety of situations. One day during a family therapy session in my office, the couple's 5-year-old son accidentally bumped his knee pretty hard. As the tears well up in his eyes, he and I had this brief interchange:

Dr. Paul: Joey, I bet that really hurts.

Joey: (Nods in agreement.)

Dr. Paul: And I bet you think it's going to hurt for a long time. ["yes" set]

Joey: (Again nods in agreement.)

Dr. Paul: And will you let me know when it hurts exactly half as much as it does right now? ["yes" set with the implied expectation that at some point in the future it will only hurt half as much]

Joey: (Again nods in agreement.)

With this, Joey turned back to his play and I resumed talking with his parents. Less than a minute later he tapped my elbow.

Joey: Dr. Paul, it only hurts half as much now.

Dr. Paul: Wow, that was quick! Thank you for telling me. And will you tell me again when it hurts exactly half as much as it does right now? [continuing with the "yes" set and the implicit expectation that the pain will continue to subside]

Joey: (Again nods in agreement.)

You can guess what happened less than a minute later. I repeated the process one more time, this time asking him to let me know when his knee felt "completely better." It wasn't long before he proudly told me that this, too, had taken place.

Dr. Paul: That's wonderful, Joey! And I wonder if you already knew that your body knows how to help you feel better that *quickly* while you continue to have fun playing?

Yes, and...

By using *and* instead of *but,* you can help create a bridge between what is already true for the other person and what he or she would like to believe is true or can become true. I helped Joey bridge what he knew was true – that his knee hurt a lot – with what he hoped would be true – that it would soon stop hurting. If you've already read Chapter 1, you probably recognized that my final request avoided the word *hurt.* Instead, I replaced it with the mental image of what I wanted him to experience: feeling completely better. Asking your child, "Does it still hurt?" invites her to search for any residual pain. A much more neutral question would be, "How do you feel now?" You can convey a more positive expectation with a question like, "How much better are you feeling now?" In the book Frogs Into Princes, Richard Bandler and John Grinder caution that "the meaning of your communication is the response that you get.

If you can notice that you're not getting what you want, change what you're doing."

Like the other language traps in this book, this one is a reminder that if you keep doing what didn't work last time, you can expect to keep getting the same results! Changing your language habits can be as challenging as changing your behavioral habits. Yet with practice, the new language habits can become as enduring, and will certainly be much more endearing.

> "If you can notice that you're not getting what you want, change what you're doing."

CHAPTER 9

TRY NOT TO TRY TOO HARD

"Sam, will you please try to mow the lawn this weekend?" "Try not to get jelly on your new shirt." "Try to get home on time tonight." "Just try a few bites." Who would suspect such a simple, three letter word of being capable of wrecking such predictable havoc in ordinary conversation? *Try* sentences are typically quite specific. There is little or no ambiguity in what is being requested. How is it, then, that such well constructed thoughts can so reliably produce exactly the opposite outcome?

The problem is one of expectations. Just as "taking the Fifth Amendment" has come to mean that the person probably has something to hide, for most people the word *try* seems to have taken on a meaning of "attempt but don't expect to succeed." Let's take a closer look at the first example above. You can imagine that Sam's response was something like, "Sure, Susan, I'll try to get it done." Now notice your own prediction about how the lawn will look by the end of the weekend. If Susan complains because it wasn't mowed, Sam's reply is likely to be a list of excuses prefaced by, "But I only said I'd try to do it."

The built-in ambiguity of this connotation of *try* has made it a common one to use in social situations in which one has been asked to do something and is unwilling to deal with the consequences of an honest answer of, "No." Most of us are familiar with this kind of two sentence interaction:

Denise: Will you be at the meeting on Friday?

Sandra: I'll try to get there.

Sandra has just politely told Denise, "Don't expect me to be there. I really don't want to go to the meeting, and I don't want to have to defend or justify my priorities with you." If she had told Denise the truth, it might have sounded more like this: "No, I won't." However, this often leads to the dreaded follow up question that contains two language traps: "Why not?" (If you've read Chapter 1 on *not* and Chapter 5 on *why*, you'll understand what I mean.) If Sandra wants to avoid getting into a discussion in which she has to explain or defend her reasons, she is likely to retreat to the more socially acceptable way of telling Denise that she won't be there, "I'll try." Denise is much less likely to ask her what might get in the way of Sandra attending the meeting. Over the years, I confess I've actually shown up at a few meetings after telling the other person I'd "try" to get there. In each case, the person in Denise's position responded to my presence with surprise, "You're here!" This reaction confirmed that my earlier response, "I'll try," had effectively conveyed the expectation, "I'll attempt to get there, but I don't expect to succeed."

If you want to have some fun experimenting with the power of *try*, ask a friend to do the experiment in the box with you. The wording of the instructions is critical, so be careful to read them exactly as written.

An experiment to try with a friend

I enjoy demonstrating the power of *try* at workshops with this two-part exercise.

Part one:

Have someone sit in an ordinary chair with both feet on the floor. Place your hands on the person's shoulders from behind and press down gently as you give the following instruction. The wording is important. Do not change it. "As you let all of your attention focus on the weight of my hands as they push down on your shoulders, try to stand up." Continue to push straight down gently as the person tries to stand up. In large groups only about one in 10 people is able to successfully stand up!

Part two:

With the same placement of your hands, this time give the following instruction. "After noticing the warmth of my hands, let all of your attention focus on your hips. Now, go ahead and stand up." With this instruction, people quickly lean forward and stand up.

The first instruction makes use of two subtle language cues. The use of the word "down" implies that the solution involves pushing "up" against the weight of your hands. However, if your feet remain in front of you when you're seated, it is impossible to stand up by moving your shoulders straight "up." The second cue was the use of the word "try" with its implied expectation that the person will not succeed.

The second instruction embeds three cues that facilitate success. In order to stand from a sitting position, you have to get your center of gravity directly over your feet. You do this by rotating at the hips. The "weight" of the hands has been replaced by a benign message of warmth. The third cue again focuses on expectations. "Go ahead and stand up" implies that you fully expect the person to succeed.

The antidote to this language trap is one of the easiest ones to implement. Most of the time the solution is no more complicated than eliminating *try to* from the sentence. "Will you please try to mow the lawn this weekend?" becomes, "Will you please mow the lawn this weekend?" "Please try to get home on time tonight." becomes, "Please get home on time tonight."

50

For those sentences in which *to* doesn't follow *try*, simply replace it with a different verb. For example: "Please try a few bites" becomes "Please have a few bites." Sometimes when I ask new clients to experiment with something the following week, they say, "I'll try." When this happens, I quickly interrupt them and say, "Please don't try." I offer them alternative phrases that have connotations of (progressive) success such as these:

- I'll work at it.
- I'll play with it.
- I'll experiment with it.
- I'll do it and notice what happens.

Am I proposing that we eliminate the word *try* from the dictionary altogether? No. There are two uses of the word that I like. The word has a genuinely unbiased, neutral expectation when combined with the word "on." When my wife asks our son to "try on a new shirt," she is conveying that she doesn't know the outcome; she doesn't know how well it will fit him. The expression, "try it on for size" similarly conveys a more neutral expectation about the outcome. In my experience, the expression seems to convey the message, "I hope this [idea] will work, though I'm not sure it will. If it doesn't, we'll keep looking for one that will work." Again, the embedded expectation is one of eventual success.

The other time that I like to use *try* is when I'm dealing with someone who is being quite stubborn or oppositional. In those situations I combine it with *don't* in a classic form of reverse psychology. Several years ago I worked with a man for whom it was very important to always be in control. He had a very difficult time accepting suggestions or ideas from other people. Knowing that he prided himself on his excellent analytical skills, I described an experiment I wanted him to undertake. Just as I finished, I feigned having second thoughts about it.

> Name two classic TV commercials in which the word try was central to the ad's theme. (Answers on page 53)

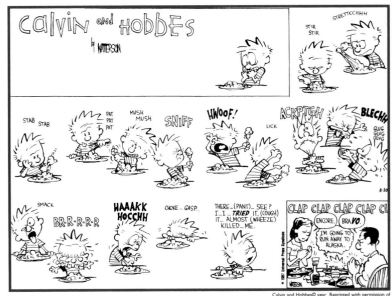

I apologized for not having adequately thought through the implications of what I was asking him to do. I concluded by saying, "Try not to think about what I said." When he returned for his next session a week later, he proudly described the success he had had with the experiment, and that obviously I had been mistaken in thinking he would be unable to handle it.

If your children have been trying your patience when you ask them to *try*, go ahead and play with this simple language change. The small shift in words will convey a big shift in your expectations. Since people often live <u>down</u> to the expectations of others, you'll help those around you by conveying your confidence that they will succeed at the projects they undertake.✳

I hope you found that the suggestions on these pages have begun to help you avoid many of the classic language traps that I've described. As I cautioned at the outset, be patient with yourself. Language habits can be just as tenacious and resistant to change as other well-ingrained habits. Involving family or good friends can help keep the process playful. Learning is easier when it's fun. Good conversations are well worth the effort.

Answers to the trivia quiz:
1. The famous Life® cereal ad that featured "Mikey".
2. One of the classic Alka Seltzer® ads used the line, "Try it, you'll like it."

Feel free to send me a brief anecdote that describes how one of these suggestions helped you to stop sabotaging a good conversation. Periodically I'll post some of the ones I receive on the web site. You may e-mail yours to **drschenk@drpaulschenk.com** or use the feedback form on the web site at **www.drpaulschenk.com/goodconversations.htm**

For postal mail, please send your anecdote to:

Dr. Paul W. Schenk
3589 Habersham at Northlake
Tucker, GA 30084-4009

©Baby Blues Partnership

GREAT WAYS TO SABOTAGE A GOOD CONVERSATION

Order Online at www.drpaulschenk.com

(Please print)

NAME: _____

ADDRESS: _____

_____

CITY: _____

STATE: _____ ZIP: _____ - _____

PAYMENT: ☐ CHECK _____

☐ VISA _____

☐ MASTERCARD _____

CARD # _____ - _____ - _____ - _____

EXPIRATION DATE: _____ / _____

NAME AS IT APPEARS ON THE CARD:

_____

(SIGNATURE) _____

| $ _____ . _____ | please send me ____ books @ $11.75 each |

| $ _____ . _____ | 7 % sales tax for Georgia residents |

| $ _____ . _____ | Shipping and handling ($2.00 for 1st book, $1.00 for each add'l book) |

| $ _____ . _____ | Total |

Dr. Paul W. Schenk earned his doctorate in Clinical Psychology from Baylor University in 1978, one of the first graduate schools in the country to offer the Doctor of Psychology (Psy.D.) degree. He provides psychotherapy for individuals (children/ teens/adults), couples and families, and conducts seminars and workshops for lay and professional groups. His articles have appeared in magazines and professional journals in the US and England. Professional memberships include the American Psychological Association, the Georgia Psychological Association (Fellow), the International Society for the Study of Dissociation, and the American Society of Clinical Hypnosis (Approved Consultant). Dr. Schenk maintains a private practice in Atlanta.